Your Invisible Magnet:

The Law of Attraction for Kids

By

Levert Jackson

A Note From The Author

As a Child, I realized that there were a lot of wonderful things in life that I wanted to have and achieve. I knew that there had to be a key to having what I wanted in life that I just did not know yet. Seeing others living their dreams made me realize, that I could live mine too. I decided that I was going to go on an adventure, a mission of sorts. I was determined to meet as many people as I could that were living their dreams, and learn how they did it. Once I discovered the key to achieving dreams, I was going to share it with other kids, teenagers and adults so that they could live their dreams too.

The truth is that we are the authors of our own life. We write what is on the pages of our own book. What we think about, we can bring about in our own life. Sometimes those ideas and thoughts come to us immediately, other times it can take a while, but they are on their way to us the moment that we begin to think it.

We write our own story. No matter what it is that we want in life, we can create it through using specific keys. These keys really do unlock the door to our own future. You can attract anything that you want in your life when you use the right keys.

First, you have to constantly think about what you want. You need to believe that you can have it. Those who believe that they can have what they want spend time envisioning it in their minds. They take the time to imagine what it feels like to have it. They know that it is coming to them, it is on the way.

They keep their minds open to the pathways that open for them to achieve it. Once the doors of opportunity open, they do not hesitate to go through them. They know that this is the door they were waiting to have open, and they step through with full confidence that they are heading straight for the life that they have already written.

It is important to think positive about what you want. What we put out into the universe will create a response. Focusing on what we don't want is not going to be as powerful as focusing on what we do want. When we focus on what we want, the faster the universe will bring it to us. We must envision a positive universe. A universe that loves us and is just waiting to give us what we need and want. Whatever we send out into the universe creates a ripple effect that will come back to us bringing along with it our desires and wants.

It is important to live your story. By living your story, you will make choices with your wants in mind. You will live as if it is already so. This means taking action. You will act upon your positive thoughts, and focus on moving towards what you want, while at the same time knowing and believing that what you want is coming to you. Eventually, you and what you want will unite at the right time and the right place.

The next step is to have an abundance of gratitude. Be grateful for what you already have. Be grateful for what is coming to you. The more grateful you are, the more that you will find to appreciate in your life. That positive energy into the universe will bring even more of what you want to you.

Additionally, it is important to give. Because you have been given so much, you need to give to others. When we give to others, the universe responds by giving even more to us. As we give and are grateful, what we really desire is moving closer to us and at a faster pace.

"All our dreams can come true, if we have the courage to pursue them."

~ Walt Disney ~

Your Invisible Magnet:

The Law of Attraction for Kids

Main Characters

Narrator: **Dad**, an inspiring man full of wisdom. He is a strong motivator who encourages his children to be successful.
Mom: **Sonia**, a loving mother, who recently had to move to another state to attend medical school.
Daughter 1: **Hannah**, the caring and logical eleven-year-old girl
Daughter 2: **Sa'de**, the artistic and skeptical eleven-year-old girl
Son: **Joshua**, the inquisitive and curious nine-year-old boy

Character Development

Each child has a distinct personality with unique inclinations, perspectives, and approaches. The readers can identify themselves under various conditions of growth and development. It allows them to see a reflection of their self-image, to predict how they will respond to similar situations and challenges.

Dad, the narrator, is an amazing father. He guides his children in bringing their best to the decision-making processes, no matter how simple the goals are. He is the binding element in the story.

Agreement

I, ______________________________________, hereby commit myself to:

- read this book.
- finish every mind exercise.
- complete each assignment.
- accomplish my daily tasks.
- fulfill my goals.

with

- confidence
- honesty
- enjoyment
- appreciation
- responsibility

because

I believe in the greatness of people;

I believe in the goodness of things around me;

I believe that My Invisible Magnet will attract all things positive; and most importantly,

I believe in ME!

Signed this _____ of _________________ in the year _______.

Witnessed by _______________________________________

(Print name and sign)

Table of Contents

"A strong, positive self-image is the best possible preparation for success."

~ Joyce Brothers ~

Guide for Parents and Guardians

Within every one of us is the ability to use positive affirmations, visualization and gratitude to fulfill our dreams and be happy- and your child is no exception. He or she has the powerful ability to shape their life, in fact maybe more so than adults, due to the force of creativity which every child has in abundance. You see, children don't have the inhibitions that we "grown-ups" have- to them anything is possible. Children are brilliant manifestors as they don't have that nagging voice in their head saying "Hey, don't you know that's impossible?", that we seem to develop as we get older. Children have the ability to daydream and believe that the impossible can be possible. As the parent, it is your responsibility to encourage these dreams and aspirations as these are the seeds that inspire and motivate individuals to succeed.

If you are not currently familiar with the Law of Attraction then I recommend that you read through this book and also familiarize yourself with other books on this topic first to fully comprehend the message that is being taught to your child. I implore you to work with your child as they undertake this journey of self-empowerment to ensure that they make the most of this book. Encourage your child to ask questions as this helps with the learning process. Don't worry if you don't know the answer straight away, be honest with your child and tell them that you don't have all the answers but you can find out together. Remember, this book is only an introduction on the Law of Attraction to your child so it is essential that you, as the parent, continue your child's learning even after you have finished the book.

Good luck and positive thinking!

Chapter One
Programming Self-Image

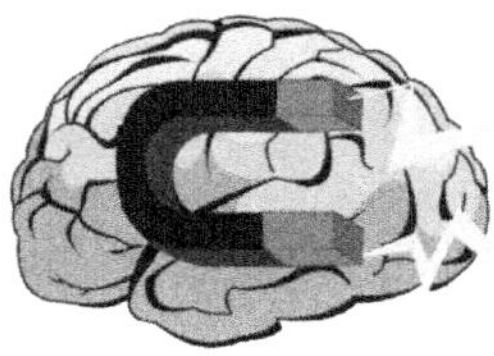

Introduction

One Saturday night in December, I came home from work with a huge pizza for dinner. As I turned the key to open my apartment door, three young voices shouted gleefully, "Surprise! Happy Birthday, Daddy!" All three kids gave me a huge hug.

"Wow, what an amazing surprise! This is great! I appreciate your effort to save up for this birthday present. Thank you!" I said, indeed very happy to see them.

Hannah, my eldest, eleven years old, beamed, "We love you, Dad! Josh, Sa'de and I wanted to get you a new shirt. Now, it is finally here."

"We saved for a year and we all planned to make it happen. I am sure you will love this, Dad." My second daughter, Sa'de, also eleven years old remarked.

Joshua, my youngest child, who is always the inquisitive one said, "Guess what, Dad? I got to practice my math. They asked me to add our money together, and subtract the amount for your birthday present. Dad, I really enjoyed saving our money and counting it. We finally chose the best shirt for the best dad in the world."

"That is great!" I said. "I am glad that you are all so thoughtful! Listen, I have a wonderful surprise present for each of you," I said. All three children beamed with happiness and embraced me.

In this scenario, Sa'de, Hannah and Josh have just used their inner ***Invisible Magnet*** and applied **The Law of Attraction.** They wished and planned for their dad's birthday present. After taking steps to make their wish a reality, they were able to achieve it.

So what is this *Invisible Magnet*? How is it related to the Law of Attraction? Let's continue to read and find out.

What is the *Invisible Magnet*?

In the dining room, my children were enjoying a slice of chocolate cake and patiently awaiting their surprise present. I came back, holding three books in one hand and a giant magnet in the other.

Joshua beamed in excitement, "Is that our surprise present, Dad? What is it?"

Hannah, who was all ears, smiled and said, "I am pretty sure it is something fantastic and exciting to read!"

"This is the magical book called *Your Invisible Magnet*," I replied. "I want each of you to read it," I explained as I gave each of my children a copy of the magic book.

As Sa'de received her copy, she said, "Dad, can I use it as a diary or something? I noticed that there are blank pages with the word *Notes* on it."

"I will explain the big secret to this magical book," I promised. Listen carefully to every word," I told them. "Never forget what I am about to tell you," I advised.

Holding the giant "U" magnet, I tried to explain how to use the book. "Look at this huge magnet," I said, holding it up for them to see. "It is attracted to iron, nickel, and steel. Imagine yourself having an *Invisible Magnet* inside your body. Think of this *Invisible Magnet* attracting a lot of things—both good and bad. If you could control this *Invisible Magnet*, what would you want to attract around you? Good things or bad things?" I asked.

Hannah raised her right hand and answered that she would definitely choose to attract good things while Sa'de was frowning as she told everyone that magnets were not concerned with whatever they attracted. I affirmed Sa'de's observation.

"Real magnets attract metals. See how this one sticks to the refrigerator?" I asked, demonstrating. "Sa'de is right; the magnet does not care what it sticks to, so long as it is metal. You *Invisible Magnet* is the same in the way that it is attracted to what you think, no matter whether it is good or bad. The *Invisible Magnet* that you have inside you can be programmed to control what you want to attract," I declared.

Pondering this, Joshua asked, "How can I control my *Invisible Magnet*, Dad?"

"You can control your *Invisible Magnet* by learning how to use The Law of Attraction," I said as I smiled at Josh, my nine-year-old son. As expected, Joshua asked what The Law of Attraction was, his face full of curiosity.

I cleared my throat and began to explain the concept. I explained in the simplest way possible, "The Law of Attraction is an idea that you can attract into your life various people, things, and situations—whether good or bad. The Law of Attraction states, that whatever you think and feel about is what you are going to get."

Sa'de was not quite sure if she understood her father and so she blurted, "So, if I think of failure, I will be doomed to fail. Is that right, Dad?"

I nodded and explained further, "Your thoughts and feelings can be good or bad ones. The Law of Attraction does not really care."

Hannah, who was listening intently, was also wondering if she truly understood what I was talking about. She whispered, "So, if I always feel sad, there is a tendency that I will attract sad things in my life? But if I am always happy then I will attract things and people who make me happy. Is that right, Dad?"

"That's correct, Hannah!" "The Law of Attraction says that you will most likely get what you desire, if you always feel and think about it. On the other hand, if there is anything you do not really want and you feel bad about, and yet you often think about it, then you will probably get it, too!"

"I do not really want to be alone and I often think of being alone. Does that mean I will be alone, Dad?" Joshua asked as he took a sip of his water.

I placed the "U" magnet on the refrigerator as I answered Josh, "Well, The Law of Attraction is a theory that says you can attract anything you often think about. This is because of the *Invisible Magnet* inside you-- which you can control," I added.

Joshua demanded, "Wait, Dad. I am confused. I can control my *Invisible Magnet* by using The Law of Attraction? How does it work?"

Sa'de smiled and told Joshua that she had an idea. She explained, "Think of it this way: Everything around us and even inside our body is some form of electromagnetic energy that can send information to one another."

Joshua frowned, a look of confusion spreading over his face. Hannah added, "It means that what is happening inside our body can create what is happening outside because of the electromagnetic power in our brain. The other day I learned in my science class that our brains are wired up with billions of neurons which are tiny cells in our bodies. Billions of them are found in the brain. They process and send information so we can think, feel, move, and live."

Suddenly, they heard thunder rumbling. Everybody looked towards the window as the lightning flashed.

Sa'de continued, "Every time we think, neurons fire up in the brain, like the lightning outside, and create magnetic fields. Therefore, our mind is like an electromagnet. When we think of what we want in our life, it will attract the things we see in our mind."

Joshua was startled. Hearing the frightening sound of the thunder, he asked, "So, our thoughts give power to our *Invisible Magnet*? How can neurons help me control my *Invisible Magnet*? I want to attract good things and not bad things."

"Every thought we have is connected to a group of neurons in our brains. If you think of something that you cannot do, then your neurons group together and tell one another that you cannot do it. Thus, you end up not doing it," Sa'de replied.

Hannah added as she tried to untie the window curtains, "Or the opposite, which is thinking that we can do it or we can have what we want. The electromagnetic energy inside us allows our neurons to connect and tell one another that we can do it or we can have it."

Everybody started to clear the small dining table and headed to the kitchen to wash the dishes. I said, "The secret of being able to do the things you want lies in what you think. YOU are the *Invisible Magnet*. Everything starts inside your head. What you think will determine what you can do. You can use The Law of Attraction to attract good things into your life by always thinking positively and maintaining happy thoughts. These beautiful thoughts will make your neurons connect and tell one another that you can have what you hope for. Your powerful mind (which is your *Invisible Magnet*) will continue to attract good things into your life to make you a better person."

The *Invisible Magnet* is within YOU! It is your electromagnetic mind. Your thoughts give your brain the power to attract things, people, and events. It can be a little confusing for now to understand fully what your *Invisible Magnet* can do for you and how you can use it by understanding The Law of Attraction. Read on and you will have a clear picture of how amazing this *Invisible Magnet* is and what it can do to help you become successful.

Are YOU ready to learn how you can control your *Invisible Magnet* and use the Law of Attraction?

Your Self-Image and The Law of Attraction

Sa'de, Hannah, Joshua and Dad gathered in the small living room while Maria Carey's *"All I Want for Christmas"* was playing softly, filling the room of the four-storey apartment with mellow sound. Each child, holding his or her magical book, was very excited to start reading.

We all were sitting on the sofa, when Joshua asked, "Dad, how can I attract good things with my *Invisible Magnet*? I really want to be successful when I grow up—just like you."

I replied, "Before you can start attracting good things with your *Invisible Magnet* you need to know yourself. The way you look at yourself is called your self-image."

Sa'de, who was sitting opposite her brother, scanning through the pages of the book, chimed in, "I learned from class, yesterday, that I can use my self-image as a tool for success. I am not sure how to do that."

"Oh, I think we can use our *Invisible Magnet*, our brain! The Law of Attraction says: if we always think about something, we will be able to attract it into our lives. So, if we think of ourselves as successful people, then we can be successful in the future. Right, Dad?" Hannah asked as she closed her magic book.

"That is right, Hannah," I replied. "Always remember, Sweetie: Everything starts with you. When I was eleven years old, like you, I used to think of growing up to be a successful and happy man. Now, I am very happy and I am successful. I have three intelligent children who will be the best persons they can be."

"That is great, Dad! That means we can choose what to attract with our *Invisible Magnet* - : our thoughts," Sa'de happily concluded.

Your self-image defines and limits what you can do. This means that if you look at yourself as someone who can attract good things into your life, then you will be able to do it. If you see yourself as a "wimp", or you are unable to use your *Invisible Magnet* properly, then you limit yourself the chance to become successful. That means you start by knowing who you are. You will not know what kind of things to attract with your *Invisible Magnet* or your thoughts, if you do not know what you like and what you do not like. Everything begins in your mind. The *Invisible Magnet* is inside your head. You can attract good things by thinking about what you like.

Think about it. Believe it, and You Can Achieve It. Let us take a look at the first part of your book tomorrow and what it can do to help you become a veterinarian someday. Sleep well son," I said as I closed the bedroom door.

Now you understand that you cannot separate what you think from who you are. Who you are is what you think and thinking comes from your brain. Be aware of what you already have inside you such as your talents. What makes up things are: your thoughts, concepts, and the information you get from outside. Only you can see what you believe. That is how your brain is wired. Go out there without fear and create a reality. You will free your self-image by saying, "I am what I decide to be." To help you find your self-image, try the following mind exercises. Turn the page now.

Mind Exercise 1: Sentence Completion
Set A

I am ____________________
(Write one word to describe yourself)

I love to ___________________
(Write one thing you enjoy doing)

I do not like ______________________
(Write one thing you dislike the most)

When I grow up, I want to be

____
(Write down your dream job)

I want to be someone like

____
(Write down one person who inspires you)

My favorite book character is ____________________
(Write the name of the book character)

because _________________________________
(Why do you like that character?)

My favorite subject in class is ______________________

My two favorite hobbies are _____________________ and

____

Set B

The Law of Attraction states that

____

____

____

____

____

The *Invisible Magnet* is

____

____

Self-image is

____

____

If I were somebody else, I would describe

____________________ (your name) as

______________________________ and

_________________________________.

Mind Exercise 2: Role Models

Paste a photo of your favorite role model or someone you admire. Write on the space provided why you like that person.

Paste your role model's photo here

____

Paste your role model’s photo here.

____

Paste your role model's photo here.

Paste your role model's photo here.

Mind Exercise 3: Diary Corner

Talk about yourself in five sentences.

Dear Diary,

Three things that I am thankful for today:

1. ______________________________________
2. ______________________________________
3. ______________________________________

Three things that I am good at:

1. ______________________________________
2. ______________________________________
3. ______________________________________

Three good things I did today:

1. ______________________________________
2. ______________________________________
3. ______________________________________

"First say to yourself what you would be; and then do what you have to do."

~ Epictetus ~

Chapter Two

Goal Setting

Vision and The Law of Attraction

On Sunday morning, the three children woke up early to help with the household chores and prepare breakfast before we went to church together.

Joshua yawned and asked, "Dad, I have a question."

"Sure, Son," I encouraged. "What is it?" I encourage my son to ask questions all the time.

"I learned last night that I can program and control my *Invisible Magnet* and that it is powered by my thoughts and my dreams," Joshua stated.

"Well, even your doubts can affect your *Invisible Magnet*, Son," I responded. "So you have to learn how to choose your thoughts carefully."

"Yeah, I will, Dad," Joshua promised. "I just need to know how my *Invisible Magnet* can attract the things I want when it cannot be seen. What if I have bad dreams? I cannot control bad dreams, Dad. What if I fail or die in my dreams? Does that mean it will come true?" Joshua asked, worried.

"You do not have to make your *Invisible Magnet* seen by others. This *Invisible Magnet* is in your mind. It is powered by your thoughts, dreams, doubts, and even your fears. You have to visualize things, people, and events by thinking about them. You have to believe in The Law of Attraction. Just like The Law of Gravity. You do not see it either, but you believe it," I reminded him.

I dropped an egg into a bowl hard enough for it to make a cracking sound. "See what happened to this egg?" I asked Josh. When I let go, it fell out of my hand and into the bowl. Why didn't it fly into the air?" I asked.

Joshua replied earnestly, "Because of gravity, Dad."

"Did you see gravity working to make the egg fall into the bowl?" I asked.

"No, I didn't," Joshua answered.

"That is how The Law of Attraction works. You have to believe it. Your bad dreams are part of your subconscious mind over which you have no full control. It does not mean that they will come true. There are dreams that you can control. These types of dreams can become reality. You have to start by setting goals," I declared.

Hannah and Sa'de gathered in the kitchen with a bottle of cooking oil and six eggs from the grocery store just two blocks from our apartment.

As I prepared the frying pan onto the stove, I said, "Alright, kids! Let me ask each of you to state one goal for today. Make sure they are S-M-A-R-T," I explained, counting off the five letters on my fingers:

S- specific,

M- measurable,

A- attainable,

R- realistic, and

T- time-bound."

Joshua got off his chair and stood beside me. "I'll go first!" he exclaimed. "My goal for today is to learn how to cook sunny side up eggs!"

Sa'de smiled as she placed the other three eggs into the refrigerator and said, "Within two hours, I shall be able to finish cleaning the living room and our bedroom."

Hannah started to set the small wooden dining table and added, "Mine is to do the laundry and clean the bathroom within two hours."

"That is great! Let's make these S-M-A-R-T goals happen within the time limits. I will teach Josh how to cook sunny side up eggs," I offered. "You girls can start doing your chores after breakfast. Make sure all of you are finished by ten o'clock so we are in time for church." I was amazed at how quickly my children had set their S-M-A-R-T. goals.

Affirmation and The Law of Attraction

We always walk to church which is just a ten-minute walk from our apartment. After locking the apartment door while everyone waited in the hallway, I said, "Our road game today is called, *Goal setting.* All you need to do is say one short-term goal and one long-term goal. Make sure they are S-M-A-R-T goals so you will not be disappointed. Are you game for that?" I asked them.

"Sure, Dad! My short-term goal is to get excellent scores on my exams this week. My long-term goal is to become a famous, professional dancer," Hannah answered. She tip-toed along the hallway, acting out hip-hop ballet dancing similar to the *Step Up* movies she had seen.

Sa'de was looking like an elegant, little princess in an old, red dress she received two years ago as a birthday present from her grandma. She responded, "My short-term goal is to win the Spelling Bee Competition this week. My long-term goal is to become a great fashion designer with my own label, *SA'DE*," she stated as she gestured in the air with her left hand as if reaching at the design label she envisioned.

My heart was touched looking at my daughters. They continuously inspire me and make me proud.

"And what about you Josh?" I asked my son. "Do you now know what you would like to be when you grow up?" I turned to my son.

"Yes, Dad. I want to be a veterinarian," Joshua said, smiling up at me with eyes full of enthusiasm.

"Great!" I enthused. "How about your short-term goal?" I smiled back.

"Hmm," Josh considered carefully. "I think my short-term goal for now is to make it to the basketball team tryouts. They are going to be on Wednesday and there are a lot of us trying out," he explained, with a worried expression.

"Don't worry Josh! I am positive you will make it," Hannah patted him on the back.

"Me too, Josh. Remember your *Invisible Magnet*?" Sa'de smiled at him.

"Oh yeah! I will think positively so I can attract good things. I will tell myself that I will make it." Joshua's eye lit up.

"That's my boy affirming that you can do it," I encouraged. "I am proud of you, Josh. No matter what!" I assured him.

Congratulations! You have just unlocked the secret of using your *Invisible Magnet* effectively. Creating a vision or setting a goal will give you a sense of direction. You need to think of what you want to happen in your life and then you need to do something about it. Make sure that your goals are sincere, precise, and consistent with your self-image. Sincerely want and commit to your goals. Make sure that they are clear and precise. Do not forget that they must fit your self-image or the way you see yourself. Complete the exercises that follow so that you will be able to apply what you have learned.

Mind Exercise 1: Creating S-M-A-R-T goals

My Long-Term Goals:

Five to ten years from now, I shall:

____

____

____

____

____

____

Paste or draw an image of you now.

Paste or draw an image of you ten years from now.

My To-Be Goals:

1.______________________________________
2.______________________________________
3.______________________________________
4.______________________________________
5.______________________________________

My To-Do Goals:

1.______________________________________
2.______________________________________
3.______________________________________
4.______________________________________
5.______________________________________

My Christmas Goals:

1.______________________________________
2.______________________________________
3.______________________________________
4.______________________________________
5.______________________________________

My New Year Goals:

1.______________________________________
2.______________________________________
3.______________________________________
4.______________________________________
5.______________________________________

Mind Exercise 2: Picture Vision

Paste pictures in the spaces that will show your goals in each of the areas below:

Family

School/Education

Christmas

Your next birthday

Mind Exercise 3: Affirmation Exercise

Some people are able to achieve what they want, while others are unable to realize even their basic desires. This is because some of us consciously program our *Invisible Magnet* using affirmations, images and visualizations. After this affirmation exercise, it is important that you back it all up with action steps every day. Positive affirmations are an important part of using The Law of Attraction.

Use the following self-statements. Say them out loud to remind you of your positive qualities and attributes. Say these affirmations every day.

"I am my own best friend."

"I can do this."

"I will never surrender."

"I am a strong person."

"I am awesome and I know it!"

"I can be successful."

"This, too, shall pass."

"I will make a difference."

"I am the change I want to see in the world."

"I have what it takes."

"I have talents and I am not afraid to share them."

"I will make it."

"I will pass this exam."

"I choose to be happy."

"I love being me."

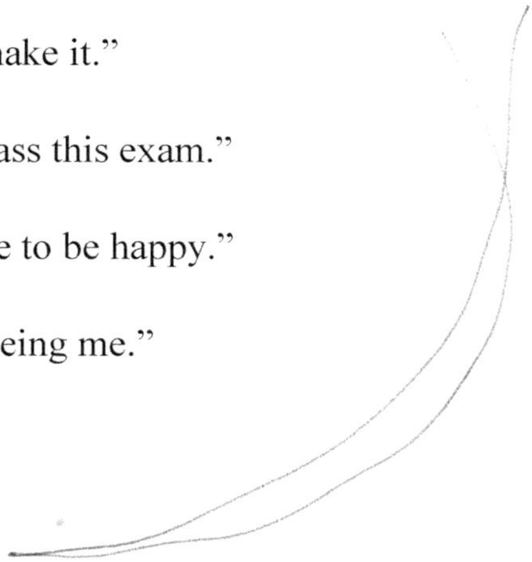

"To accomplish great things, we must not only act, but also dream; not only plan, but also believe."

~ Anatole France ~

Chapter Three

Daydreaming

Dreams, Doubts, and The Law of Attraction

"...10 seconds to go on the shot clock. He glides! He shoots! He scores...a spectacular phenomenon! What a move by Joshua Jackson..." The commentator echoed in the mind of Joshua as he imagined himself playing basketball wearing a crimson red uniform. Joshua felt proud of himself as his teammates hugged him happily after he made that heroic, last-second shot, complete with his fancy footwork and fantastic sky-walking abilities.

This was just a fantasy he created during his break time from class that afternoon. He did not buy snacks because he was saving money for a pair of basketball shoes which he planned to buy when he got accepted on the team. He stayed under the shady tree and daydreamed that he would be included on the basketball team that year. He ate three crackers he had brought from home and drank a glass of juice that his teacher had given him.

Suddenly, his friend, Connor, was behind him. Connor shook Joshua's shoulder, pulling him out of dreamland. Connor brought an extra pair of basketball shoes and handed them to Joshua. "Here you go, Josh! You can borrow these until you get a new pair," Connor said.

Startled by the sudden arrival of his friend, Joshua replied, "Thank you, Connor."

"You're welcome," Connor responded. He covered his mouth as he sneezed. "Hey, Josh, are you scared about the tryouts this afternoon?" Connor asked.

"A little," Joshua admitted. "What about you?" Joshua asked his friend.

"Oh, I think I am not going to make it, Josh. I can't shoot hard enough. My mom tells me I have very short legs and I cannot run as fast as you can," Connor said. Joshua looked at Connor and thought he was lucky to have long legs that could run really fast.

"My dad tells me that being afraid is all in the mind. He said we can control our mind not to be afraid," Joshua said. He placed his right hand on Connor's shoulder and tried to encourage him.

"Oh, I don't think I can tell my mind what to think, Josh. That is really tough," Connor answered.

"You can at least try, Connor. Dad calls it The Law of Attraction," Joshua explained.

"The Law of Attraction? How does it work?" Connor wondered.

"Well, all you need to do is think good thoughts and something good will come to you," Joshua smiled.

"Oh, that sounds like magic, Josh. I do not believe in magic and I do not think I can control my thinking. I always think that I will not make it to the team this year. I cannot help it. I am just not good enough, I guess," Connor told Joshua.

"Well, you can at least give it a try, Connor," Joshua smiled. "What harm can it do?"

At dinner that night, I asked Josh how his basketball tryouts had gone. "Oh Dad, it was great! I was totally having fun and during the tryout game, I made a last ten-second score just like I had imagined it when I was daydreaming this afternoon."

"Oh, I am so proud of you," I said giving Joshua a high five. The girls clapped in sheer delight as they congratulated their little brother.

"So your *Invisible Magnet* is attracting the nice things you dreamed. Right?" Hannah winked at Joshua.

"Yeah, I guess I am taking control of my *Invisible Magnet*," Joshua answered. "Tomorrow, I will see if The Law of Attraction really works!"

"What is tomorrow, Josh?" Sa'de asked after drinking a glass of water.

"Well, the basketball coach promised to post the list of those who made it to the team this year and I think ...well, I believe, I made it. I mean, I want to believe I made it, you know," Joshua said trying to convince himself that he really succeeded.

"Let us know tomorrow, then," I said. "Keep your *Invisible Magnet* and The Law of Attraction working."

The next day, Connor ran along the lobby towards Joshua who was getting his basketball shoes from the locker.

"Congratulations, Josh! You did it! You made the team this year!" Connor announced.

"What? I made it? Let me see the list," Joshua exclaimed, excited.

The boys ran towards the bulletin board where the coach had posted the names of those who made the team. Joshua jumped for joy after seeing his name on the list.

"Wait," Joshua said suddenly, as looking for his friend's name. There was no Connor on the list.

Connor looked sad but not surprised. "I told you," he said. "I knew I wasn't going to make it. I need more practice."

"Oh, I am sorry, Connor," Joshua said.

"It is okay. I knew it already," Connor replied.

"I think you just need to believe in yourself," Joshua added. "My dad told me that everything starts in yourself—even our successes. So try again and next time you have to believe it. Then, you will make it."

Joshua announced his success to me that night. He explained how he truly believed in The Law of Attraction and his power to control his *Invisible Magnet*. We were all delighted to hear him talk about his basketball tryout and his evidence-based discovery about The Law of Attraction and the power of his *Invisible Magnet*.

Joshua learned that dreams and doubts can trigger the *Invisible Magnet* to turn on The Law of Attraction. He realized that he was attracting positive things because he was dreaming and thinking of it all the time. His friend was very doubtful and so he attracted negative result. To Joshua, the *Invisible Magnet* works like magic and The Law of Attraction does, indeed, exist even though it is not visible just like The Law of Gravity.

Believing and The Power of your *Invisible Magnet*

One morning, just before school, Hannah and Sa'de were talking to their reflections in the mirror using positive affirmations such as "I can do this.", "I will win the spelling bee.", "I can be a great hip-hop dancer.", "I shall not be afraid." and "I will make it."

"Alright, girls!" I called out. "You will miss the school bus if you do not leave the apartment right now," I said, scanning the newspaper.

Hannah immediately took her backpack and kissed me on the right cheek saying, "On our way, Dad. See you later."

"I just turned on my *Invisible Magnet*," Sa'de added after she kissed my left cheek and happily skipped out the door.

"Me too!" Joshua said and kissed me good-bye.

At the library that same morning, Hannah was reading the giant book of dreams when she suddenly stepped into dreamland. She envisioned herself being a famous dancer entertaining guests at a music award twelve years in the future. She smiled at the thought of her entertaining people and realized that making people smile because of her talent is what she really loves to do. She would love to hear them clap and cheer for her as she danced to the tune of her favorite hip-hop music.

Suddenly, she felt a hand on her back. She was startled to hear the voice of her physical education teacher.

"Hannah, would you be interested in trying out for the cheering squad? Auditions start at five o'clock in the afternoon in the gymnasium."

Hannah blinked twice trying to be sure that she was not just dreaming. Awe struck, she replied, "Yes, Ms.

Williams, I am interested. I will be there to audition. Thank you."

Later that evening, Sa'de was cooking dinner and telling us how worried she was over the upcoming spelling bee. Although she was anxious, she believed in the power of her mind. She kept telling herself that she would win the spelling bee the day after tomorrow. She had been preparing hard for the competition. She studied every day during her break time and even at night after she completed her homework. I gave her the drills that she needed to practice and sharpen her brain. She enjoys reading and learning how to spell and pronounce new words.

Joshua blurted out, "Hey Hannah, I saw you did that dance move when you went to audition at the gym. Are you really going to be a cheerleader?"

"Oh yes, Josh! I am excited!" Hannah replied. The results will be announced this Friday. I would like to believe that I will make the team this year. It is going to be really fun!"

"I bet it will be," I said.

The kids were now using their *Invisible Magnet* to attract good things into their lives. Joshua succeeded in his basketball tryouts. He kept his thoughts simple and positive. Sa'de also won the spelling bee as she used the power of her *Invisible Magnet,* believing strongly that she would win. Hannah was also accepted to the cheerleading team this year cheering for the school's sports teams. In fact, she became the lead dancer of the group. I am truly proud of my kids.

You see, daydreaming is a healthy exercise for your *Invisible Magnet*. Use it to motivate and inspire yourself and to attract good things into your life. Remember that whatever your thoughts are, whether they are nice dreams or unpleasant doubts, you can attract them because the *Invisible Magnet* is in you. It has no ability to choose what it attracts. You have to believe that you have the power to control your mind by thinking only pleasant thoughts and putting aside your fears and doubts. Learn to use daydreaming and affirmation as healthy exercises for your mind.

How to day dream +
Visualise -

environment
what are you doing?
who with?
what do you believe
about yourself?

Mind Exercise 1: Mental Movies

Relax, play a mellow song and time yourself for fifteen minutes. Use each keyword to create a theater in your mind. Reflect/imagine situations you can relate to the following keywords:

- Past Success
- Self-Confidence
- Mentor
- Laughter
- Purpose
- Choice
- Courage
- Charity
- Forgiveness
- Alive

Theater in your Invisible Magnet

Mind Exercise 2: Indoor Reflection

Watch any or all of the following movies and write your own movie review by reflecting on how you relate to the characters. Describe what you have discovered and realized after watching the movie. You can also write what things you want to learn more about. What lessons are related to the *Invisible Magnet* and The Law of Attraction? Write ten sentences only.

A Photo of ***Meet the Robinson's*** here please

Meet the Robinson's

A Photo of ***Pay It Forward*** here please

Pay It Forward

A Photo of ***The Pursuit of Happyness*** please

The Pursuit of Happyness

A Photo of ***The Karate Kid* (2010)** here please

***The Karate Kid* (2010)**

A Photo of ***Soul Surfer*** here please

Soul Surfer

A Photo of ***Happy Feet*** here please

Happy Feet

A Photo of ***Arthur Christmas*** here please

Arthur Christmas

A Photo of ***The Secret*** here please

The Secret

(Your Favorite Movie) Title: ______________________

Mind Exercise 3: Outdoor Reflection

This is going to be an outdoor activity. Go outside over the weekend. Visit someone you know, a relative or a friend. Think of a task that you can do for that person like assisting him/her in his/her garden, or in the kitchen. Wash dishes for the person or clean his/her yard or even babysit for free. Think of something helpful. At the end of the day, take a picture with that person. When you get back home at night, write about your experience in the diary corner.

Daydreaming Phase: Go out into a quiet place and start daydreaming about a good act you can do for someone without spending a dime. Brainstorm possible ways to help. Think of a person you know like a relative or a friend who deserves something nice during the weekend.

Planning Phase: Write down your plans here. Create a goal statement about what you generally want to achieve. List the objectives of the activity that you are going to do over the weekend.

Action Phase: Take a picture with the person whom you are going to help. Write down what happened during your weekend expedition. Reflect on the goal you set and the objectives. Were they met? What have you done to make them successful? Which objectives did not go as planned and what can you do to ensure success next time?

The Diary Corner:

Paste the photo here

"Action is the foundational key to all success."

~ Pablo Picasso ~

Chapter Four
Creating Success

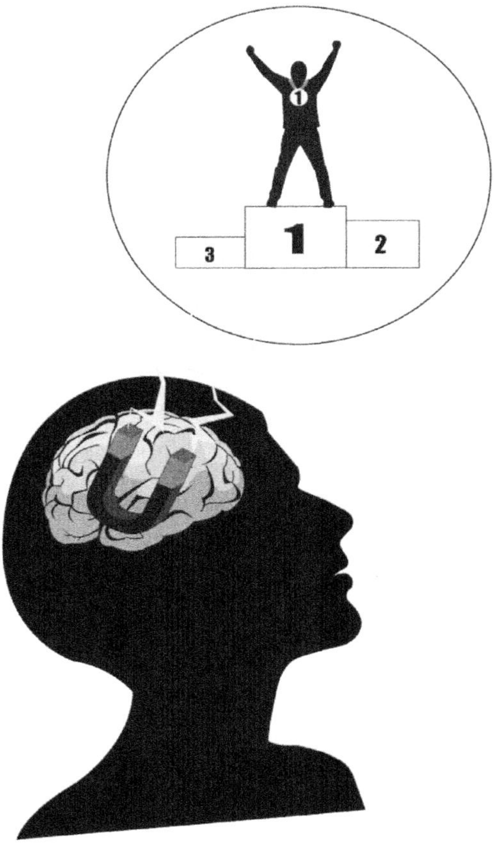

Actions Speak Louder than Words

Ding, ding, ding, ding, ding, ding!

My *Good Morning Verizon* ring tone alarm clock woke me up at six thirty one December Monday morning. I stretched my arms and opened my right eye, trying to accommodate the early morning rays of the sun coming through my bedroom window. Joshua, who was in the adjacent room, also woke up to the sound of the alarm tone and started to stretch his cotton pajama-clad legs.

"Good morning, little kid! Rise and shine! Early bird catches the worm so let's get out there and be productive!" I said as I planted my feet on the cold floor of my son's bedroom. I threw Josh a pillow to fully energize him and make him get out of the bed.

Sa'de and Hannah were already busy preparing breakfast when Josh and I entered into the dining area. We had sausages and bread that morning. Hannah made me a cup of cappuccino and Sa'de poured milk into three glasses. I unfolded the newspaper and started reading the headlines and the first-page news. The children were discussing things to do for that day Joshua and I shared a joke. The kids then kissed me good-bye before leaving the apartment. They hurried down the stairs to board the school bus, just outside the apartment.

On my way to work I whispered a prayer. Monday is usually a busy day in the bookstore. When I got there, my coworkers exclaimed, "Congratulations, Mr. Jackson!"

I was a little surprised but I responded to each of them with a smile. *What are they talking about?*" I wondered. I went straight to the office and our manager gave me a letter and shook my hand.

He said, "Congratulations, Jackson. You have been promoted to assistant manager!"

"Thanks, Mr. Allen. This is great!" I said, smiling.

"Oh, you deserve the position. I will be retiring next year and I am recommending you for the manager's position. Learn all you can. I know you will be doing great things for this bookstore," he said.

"Thank you, sir," I answered.

I could not wait for dinner time to tell my kids about the promotion. All I wanted that moment was to celebrate the good news with my children. Setting a good example as a parent is challenging. It is truly rewarding to make them see that their dad is also capable of attracting success. It is very important that children see parents as role models to being successful.

I had an orientation that morning with the whole new role and the list of tasks and responsibilities of the assistant bookstore manager. The Monday workday went by so fast with all the new tasks. When work was finally done, I hurried back to the apartment and met my kids there. I had called Hannah earlier that day and told her not to make dinner because we were going out to celebrate.

The kids were very excited to see me when I reached the apartment. "That is great, Dad! You made your *Invisible Magnet* attract a promotion at work!" Joshua cheerfully jumped up and gave me a high five. Hannah and Sa'de hugged me and said they were so proud to have a daddy like me. I could not have been any happier at that moment hearing those words from my kids.

We all walked happily to Kobe's, a restaurant just a stone's throw away from the apartment. We ate a hearty meal and I told them my success story and related it to the *Invisible Magnet* and The Law of Attraction. My story made Joshua, ultimately, more convinced in the power of his own *Invisible Magnet*.

"Now, I understand that we do not need to be successful right away. Sometimes there are trials and obstacles along the way before we succeed," Sa'de concluded after hearing my story of success and failure.

"That is reality, Sa'de. You live in an imperfect world. Anything could happen. You can fall but it is up to you to rise up once again and try," I said.

"How did you get the strength to try again, Dad after you lost your business?" Hannah asked.

"Well, it is because of the three of you, of course. You all inspire me. I cannot just let myself go down and stay there forever. Business closed. Your mom had to move to another state to attend medical school, and things have been hard for us for a while but I had to gather all the strength I needed to get back up and raise you well. You are my strength," I told them. "I cannot bear seeing your life without direction. So, here I am, starting all over again, taking action, and using my *Invisible Magnet* to attract good things into our lives. This is the secret I am sharing with you. You will have to use it properly. Okay?" I asked my children.

"Yes, Dad. We will! Promise," all three kids replied in unison.

Creating success must involve actions. It is not merely having dreams and then waiting and let those dreams come true. Nothing can come true without you acting on your dreams. It is good to plan but it is great to put those plans into actions. It is not enough just to talk about how to use your *Invisible Magnet*. You have to show people that it works by example. To be believable you must also walk the talk. This is a challenge for everyone who wants to be a great role model. That is why it is not easy to be a great parent. However, anything is possible when you know how to use your *Invisible Magnet*. Find a great role model who has been through ups and downs of life. Listen to his or her advice. He or she can be a parent, or grandparents, your teachers, or just about anyone close to you. Remember: You and your role model have to walk the talk.

"Dad, I will be coming home late tonight. I have cheer dance practice," Hannah told me.

"Okay, enjoy your dance practice and take care on your way home," I told my daughter.

"I will, Dad. Thanks!" Hannah responded.

Thirty minutes later, I got another call. This time, it was from Sa'de. "Daddy, can I join the Art Club this afternoon after class?"

"How long is the meeting?" I asked.

"Just for thirty minutes, Dad," Sa'de answered.

"Alright then, Josh and I will cook dinner tonight and we will wait for you," I said.

"Okay, Dad. Thanks." Sa'de had dreamed of becoming a famous fashion designer someday. She wanted her talent in drawing, painting, and creative fashion design to be enhanced. She had wanted to join the Art Club for some time but could not do it because of the requirements like art materials that we could not previously afford.

Joshua was becoming more driven in his basketball practice. He was always on time for practice and even watched basketball lessons on YouTube during his free time. Additionally, he also wrote for the school paper and wrote a column on Pets and Animals, his first love. Joshua also visited his Uncle Jeff on weekends to help and observe what his uncle does for the animals that need the help of a veterinarian. He even helped a stray kitten, adopted it, and named it Winter.

While cooking dinner that night, Joshua said, "Dad, I have a new game."

"What's that?" I asked.

"Guess who," Joshua answered.

"Who? What?" I asked.

"The name of the game is Guess Who," Joshua explained.

"Oh…okay. Go ahead!" I told my son.

"Alright, Dad! Guess who invented the telephone?" Joshua asked.

"Oh, that is too easy. Alexander Graham Bell," I immediately answered.

"That is correct!" Joshua smiled. "You go next, Dad. Ask me."

"Alright then, guess who created the formula: $E=mc^2$?" I waited for Joshua's answer.

"Albert Einstein!" Joshua answered in an instant.

"You got it!" I was impressed.

"Alright, Dad! Who invented this formula: The *Invisible Magnet* + The Law of Attraction = Action?" Joshua asked.

"You did, Josh! I laughed.

"That is great, Dad!" We both laughed and finished cooking. We were just setting the table as Sa'de came into the dining area.

"How's the art club, Sa'de?" Josh asked.

"Oh, it was awesome! I cannot wait to make my own fashion statement someday," Sa'de enthused. "I know I have to work hard like everybody else before I can get my own brand: SA'DE," she said, looking into the horizon visualizing herself on the runway with her models and fashion designs.

"That is awesome! When that day comes, you will have to make me one of your male models!" We all laughed at the thought of Joshua becoming one of the models for the brand that Sa'de would be designing.

"Josh, I will be joining the basketball team's uniform design contest next week. You should critique what I will make, okay? You have to be honest though," Sa'de warned her brother, "And no bias because I'm your sister!"

"Sure, Sa'de. I will be glad to help. I will be wearing those when you get to win the contest anyway and that will make me one of your models already." We laughed again and started to eat dinner.

While waiting in the living room for Hannah to come home, I reflected on the formula that Joshua had created: The *Invisible Magnet* + The Law of Attraction = Action. I smiled at the thought of a nine-year-old boy creating a formula for success. I felt proud of myself for walking the talk. It may have been a long journey but I was truly happy I had succeeded and achieved the job promotion. Nothing can be more convincing than to see results in action.

It is good to always think positively, to dream, and to plan the steps for making a dream come true. Good things will be attracted by your *Invisible Magnet* if you focus on positive, good thoughts. However, to create success, there has to be some active involvement on your part. You cannot just think and dream and let The Law of Attraction work for you. You have to act. Actions make things happen.

Hannah would not have become the lead dancer in her cheering squad if she had not prepared for it. She practiced during weekend and she watched dance shows, movies, and internet video lessons, and read self-help books.

Sa'de would not have won the Spelling Bee if she had not studied. She read a lot and did the drills. It was not magic or destiny. It was the result of a dream backed up with actions.

Joshua made it to the basketball varsity team for his age group because he did his part. He had played in the neighborhood basketball court with other kids, right after school since he was six years old. He watched Michael Jordan's games and he read books about basketball. These are all actions that provided him with results. He believed in his dreams. This, in turn, powered his *Invisible Magnet* and attracted opportunities for what he is good at. But he did not succeed just by waiting. He took action. He joined the tryouts—no matter how scary it was for him. Not having a good pair of basketball shoes did not stop him. He took action by borrowing shoes. He joined the tryouts and accepted the risk of possibly not making it to the team this year but set aside his fears and doubts. He tried again after not making it last year. He took the necessary action to realize his dream.

Inspired Action.

Mind Exercise 1: Flashback

Reflect on a small achievement of the past. Write down what made you successful in that situation. Relate it to how your *Invisible Magnet* and The Law of Attraction played a vital role in your achievement. Describe the actions you took that helped create your success.

Achievement: ______________________________

Mind Exercise 2: Hall of Success

Paste photos of celebrities. Beside each photo describe what made this person successful and list his achievements.

At the end, paste your own photo and daydream about your future achievements. List those as well.

Paste photo here

Paste photo here

Paste photo here

Paste photo here

Paste photo here

Mind Exercise 3: Mental Gymnastics

This activity will teach you how to make alternative plans. It will help you become flexible, too!

Write five to ten sentences about the things you have done to carry out your goals for the week. Write down those that you were not able to achieve, the reasons why, and the plans or steps that you can take to make those goals happen next week.

"Happiness is not something ready- made. It comes from your own actions."

~ Dalai Lama ~

Chapter Five
Choosing Happiness

Happiness: The Best Tool for Success

Some people believe that in order to be happy, one must be successful. In reality, it is the other way around. In order to be successful, you have to be happy. Happiness is a state of mind. It is a choice. The power lies in you to decide.

One Sunday afternoon at the park, Sa'de was curled up on the blanket far away from where the family gathered. She was looking at the horizon deep in thought. I walked slowly and sat beside her.

I placed her hat on her head. "What's wrong, Sweetie?" I asked.

"Nothing, Dad," she answered.

"Nothing to me seems like something," I told her. "Go on, you can tell me. Maybe I can help," I urged gently.

"I am having problems with making a decision, Dad," she confessed. "There is this Fashion Design Workshop for kids on Saturday next week but on the same day, I will be representing the Spelling Bee Inter-School Competition. I am confused. I do not know which one to choose," Sa'de confessed.

"Which of the two do you think is more important to you and will make you happier?" I asked my daughter.

"Both are important to me, Dad," she said. "If I join the Spelling Bee, I will be happy and if I join the workshop, I will also be happy. I do not know which one to choose."

"That's tough, indeed," I said. "How about we look at the situation like this: Imagine yourself not joining the Spelling Bee Competition then ask yourself if you can live with that. Then, imagine not joining the Fashion Design Workshop now. How would you feel? You will never know if you will regret it or not, until you decide and see what happens. Regrets do not come before the circumstances. You will know if it is an unwise decision for you when you regret it down the road. I will leave you for a while to think about this," I told her. "I know that you will ultimately have to choose one over the other. Choose the one that you know will truly make you happy for the rest of your life. Do not think of other things."

Sa'de smiled and hugged me as she said, "Thank you, Daddy."

Saturday came swiftly for Sa'de and she was so excited that she was not able to sleep soundly on Friday night. Wearing a small white blazer over her navy blue sleeveless dress which was given by her Aunt Tatiana for her eleventh birthday, she felt like the prettiest girl alive that day.

"Bye, Dad. I have to be on time for the workshop today," she said.

"Enjoy the seminar, Sweetie." Sa'de kissed me good-bye and headed for the Fashion Design Workshop. It was a whole-day workshop for kids, ages ten-to-thirteen years old who were joining *Project Runway for Kids* the following month, the biggest dream of Sa'de's.

Choosing happiness is not a piece of cake—especially when you are torn between two situations that you know can make you happy. Sa'de was in a dilemma because she wanted both. She knew that sacrificing one over the other would eventually give her mixed emotions. She was not sure about what she really wanted and what really fit her whole personality as well as the person that she could become in the future. With reflection and guidance, she realized that if she wants something she can't just let it happen. She will have to work towards achieving her dream. She concluded that no one can decide what she should do. She remembered that her *Invisible Magnet* must be powered by her own thoughts. Her own thoughts and rationalization, not the circumstances themselves, will justify her happiness. This means that she has the power to define her own meaning of happiness. Sacrificing one event over the other does not necessarily mean she can no longer be successful and happy for what she chooses to believe. She knows she wants to be a fashion designer when she grows up. An opportunity opened up for her, fortunately, at a very young age. She could not bear the thought of not joining the workshop over an equally important event to represent her school at the Inter-School Spelling Bee Competition. She realized that joining the Spelling Bee is important for her school but joining the Fashion Design Workshop is important to her.

Pursuing happiness does not mean one is being selfish. Choosing a circumstance in life so you can fulfill other people's happiness because you are needed is not a real, personal happiness. It will only make you feel bitter in the end and can lead to regrets. Remember that happiness is not a reward for being selfless. It is not a prize to take. It is a natural state of mind that goes with your being and your actions. Happiness is not a package that is custom built for every circumstance you face. You create it, together with whom, and what you are, your self-image, your actions, or your behaviors.

Sa'de made a wise decision. She chose happiness considering her being and knowing that acting on the circumstance would truly make her happy and not necessarily focus on making others happy. Choosing what makes you happy does not mean you are being selfish. These are two completely separate and different things.

Hannah spent her twelfth birthday raising funds to help feed the homeless instead of having a party. She organized a small "dance for a cause" in her school with the help of her cheer dance coach, the cheer dance team, and Joshua's basketball team. Hannah has the type of personality that wants to help other people. She has her own personal goals but she is also self-directed to other impersonal goals or causes which she identifies herself with.

"I want to share my talent with others, Dad," she'd explained. "I want to use it to help other people, too. It is my dream to entertain people through dancing and there is a good chance my friends' dreams can also come true when they get to show other people their talent in dancing. It will be fun and we can invite our parents to the show. The money will go to the homeless and we can share food with them on Thanksgiving Day or Christmas," Hannah said as she shared her plan with us a week before her birthday.

"I'm glad you thought of that. What a wonderful idea," I complimented her.

"Thanks, Dad." She smiled.

Having a goal and an understanding of what is involved may not be enough. One should have the courage to pursue goals and take action. Hannah clearly demonstrated that goal when she facilitated and organized the whole event in her school. She had the courage to ask for help from her teachers, Josh's basketball team, and her cheer dance team. She facilitated the needed communication and solicitation as she organized the different committees involved in the preparation for the barn dance. All these activities need courage. Hannah took the risk of committing mistakes. There was a risk of failure or humiliation. This is what it takes for one to succeed. I am proud of my daughter.

The phone rang just as we were returning to the apartment after Hannah's dance fundraiser. It was Sonia, my wife. After we talked, I called Hannah who was very eager to share with her Mom everything about her birthday celebration.

"Thank you, Mom. I am very happy," Hannah said. "We raised $3,000 for the homeless." Hannah went on to tell her mother how she prepared for the barn dance and the challenges they met before the fund-raising campaign concluding with the triumphant success of the whole event. Her mom was so proud hearing her eldest daughter's success story.

Hannah could not sleep that night reflecting on her birthday event. She was too happy to sleep so she wrote something in her diary instead. Her notes which she addressed to, "Wisdom" went like this:

Dear Wisdom,

I have just unlocked the secret to my Invisible Magnet: Happiness. I discovered that happiness is actually in our human mind. I learned that I can think better, do better, and feel better when I am happy. Well, my birthday, indeed, is a happy one. I was thinking of happy thoughts when I woke up this morning and I believe my Invisible Magnet attracted good things into my life today. The barn dance was well attended by parents, teachers, relatives, schoolmates, and friends. Everyone was entertained during the barn dance and best of all: We were able to raise an enormous amount of funds that we can use to help the homeless and the hungry. I have learned from Mom and Dad to always give back and to share my talents with others. I have also discovered that when I choose to be happy, I became a better dancer. I also feel healthier and I tend to be more charitable towards other people. My Invisible Magnet, which secretly contains happiness inside it, attracted success into my life. I think happiness is just inside our mind and it is up to us to unlock it."

Yours,
Hannah

Mind Exercise 1: HAPPINESS

According to Maxwell Maltz, happiness is not something that is earned or deserved. It is thinking of pleasant thoughts. Think of anything that makes you happy that starts with each of the letters in the word, "HAPPINESS" and write the word on the space provided.

H- ______________________________

A- ______________________________

P- ______________________________

P- ______________________________

I- ______________________________

N- ______________________________

E- ______________________________

S- ______________________________

S- ______________________________

Paste a photo of your happy face here.

Mind Exercise 2: Finding Felicity

Felicity means happiness. Finding what makes you happy can lead you to success. Finding felicity, therefore, will help you find success. Try to complete this activity and find out how these famous and successful people unlocked their Invisible Magnet and find felicity and success. Research what these people are famous for, and what happiness they had that led them to become successful.

Justin Bieber

Famous for: ________________________

Happy with: ________________________

Gabby Douglas

Famous for: ________________________

Happy with: ________________________

Leonardo da Vinci

Famous for: ________________________

Happy with: ________________________

Isaac Newton

Famous for: ________________________

Happy with: ________________________

China Anne McClain

Famous for: ________________________

Happy with: ________________________

Bella Thorne

Famous for: ________________________

Happy with: ________________________

Thomas Jefferson

Famous for: ________________________

Happy with: ________________________

Yao Ming

Famous for: ______________________

Happy with: ______________________

Mind Exercise 3: Reflection of SUCCESS

Walt Disney, who has a success-oriented personality, has the following traits:

With your *Invisible Magnet* and the Law of Attraction, you can build your personality into the success-type. Would you like that? Start building now. In completing this activity, you will discover an awesome reflection of success when you look into the mirror.

SENSE OF DIRECTION

Write down in one sentence the Personal Goal which you want to achieve in your life.

My Personal Goal:

____

____

____

Think of a project you want to finish. Write it down.

____

____

____

____

Think of a selfless goal or a cause that you want to do for others. Write it down. (Example: Feeding the homeless.)

____

____

____

____

UNDERSTANDING

Seek the truth and facts around you, the problem you face, the people you know, and even yourself. Write down on the space provided the FACTS, the information that first comes to mind after each keyword item/phrase.

My nickname: ______________________________

My weakness: ______________________________

My strength/asset: __________________________

A problem that I am facing now:

____

____

What I like BEST about my parents:

____

____

A mistake I made:

____

____

What I can do to avoid the same mistake:

COURAGE

You need to have courage in order for you to take action and make your goals and dreams become a reality.

Write down what you fear doing. Is it speaking in public? Reporting in class, or joining a competition? Write as many fears as you can.

____

____

____

____

____

____

____

____

____

Write down the fears that you have overcome and the obstacles you have surmounted.

____

____

____

____

____

____

____

____

____

____

____

Make sure to visit this page once in a while. Take note of the fears that you are now able to overcome.

CHARITY

People who are successful usually have a charitable heart and concern for others. Write down the things you appreciate in the following people:

- Your Dad:

____

____

- Your Mom:

____

____

- Your Brother/Sister:

____

____

- Your Teacher:

____

____

- Your Best Friend:

____

____

Next, stop and think about the very important people in your life. Think of what they feel, their needs, and even their dreams. Think of them for only fifteen minutes. Write down your thoughts and feelings about others in your diary corner.

The Diary Corner

____

____

____

____

____

____

____

____

ESTEEM

Continue to attract good things into your life by thinking of positive things. Create a mental picture of yourself that is happy and healthy. Again, do a mental movie for fifteen minutes, thinking only of good and happy thoughts with you starring as the great actor/actress. Follow up with a self-affirmation activity. Talk to your reflection in the mirror and telling yourself all the positive words.

SELF-CONFIDENCE

Now, you are almost done building your success personality. Add the ability to be confident. How can you do this? Think back to the past. Think of your past successes and moments of bravery. Relive those moments as you reflect. Write down at least five successful and courageous moments you can recall.

- ______________________________
- ______________________________
- ______________________________
- ______________________________
- ______________________________

Paste a photo of your successful, victorious, or brave moment here

SELF-ACCEPTANCE

Tell yourself that it is all right to be imperfect just like everyone else. Read about the following famous and successful people who also experienced failure. Write down their failure/life challenge or the obstacle they encountered and their success. The first one is done for you.

- **Michael Jordan**

Success: known as the greatest basketball player of all time
Obstacle: removed from his high school basketball team

- **Bill Gates**

Success:______________________________
Obstacle: ____________________________

- **Walt Disney**

Success:______________________________
Obstacle: ____________________________

- **Albert Einstein**

Success:______________________________
Obstacle: ____________________________

- **Thomas Edison**

Success:______________________________
Obstacle: ____________________________

- **Winston Churchill**

Success:______________________________

Obstacle: ____________________________

- **Oprah Winfrey**

Success:______________________________

Obstacle: ____________________________

- **Henry Ford**

Success:______________________________

Obstacle: ____________________________

- **Lance Armstrong**

Success:______________________________

Obstacle: ____________________________

- **Martin Luther King Jr.**

Success:______________________________

Obstacle: ____________________________

Remind yourself, time and time again, that it is okay to be imperfect. Take it from these inspiring words:

"I have missed more than 9,000 shots in my career. I have lost almost 300 games. On 26 occasions, I have been entrusted to take the game winning shot, and I missed. I have failed over and over and over again in my life. And that is why I succeed." –MICHAEL JORDAN

"Success is not final, failure is not fatal. It is the courage to continue that counts." – WINSTON CHURCHILL

"Failure is simply the opportunity to begin again, this time more intelligently." – HENRY FORD

"It's fine to celebrate success but it is more important to heed the lessons of failure." - BILL GATES

"Failure is another stepping stone to greatness."
– OPRAH WINFREY

"Feeling gratitude and not expressing it, is like wrapping a present and not giving it."

~ William Arthur Ward ~

Chapter Six
Exercising Gratitude

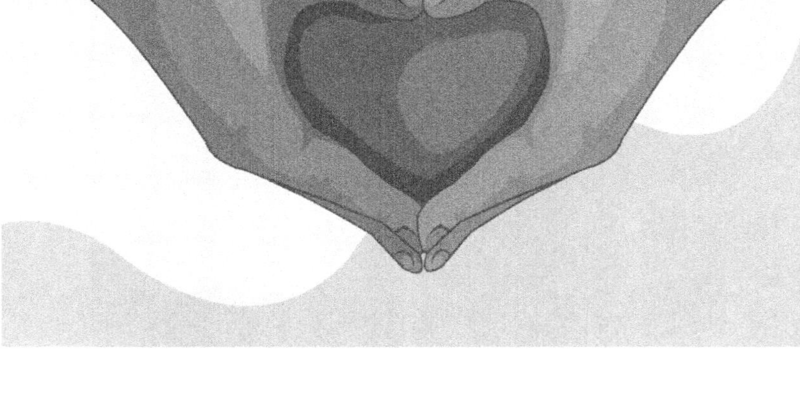

The Importance of Gratitude

Joshua had a homework assignment to list all words that say "Thank you!" in at least ten different languages. He also had an essay about Thanksgiving Day. He headed to the public library to research the different thank you words and the history of Thanksgiving.

"I will be back for lunch, Dad. My homework will not take that long," Joshua informed me one Saturday morning. Since he had begun to understand the meaning and the secret to the *Invisible Magnet*, he had become much more self-driven. He had a sense of purpose. He had started to be more systematic in time management. He had learned to balance schoolwork and basketball practice.

When Joshua got back from the public library, the girls and I were done cooking lunch. Josh was just in time to join us.

"So, how's your homework research, Josh?" Hannah asked.

"Oh, I discovered a lot of "thank you" words and some interesting information about Thanksgiving," Joshua replied, looking satisfied and proud of himself.

"Come on Josh! Share it, please. What are your research findings?" Sa'de teased Joshua.

"Well, I discovered that, in French, you say, '*Merci*'; in Chinese you say, '*Xie Xie*' (Shyeh Shyeh); in German you say '*Danke*'; in Spanish you say, '*Gracias*'; in Russian you say, '*Spasibo*'; in Portuguese you say, '*Obrigado*'; in Hawaiian you say, '*Mahalo*'; in Arabic you say, '*Shukran*'; in Japanese you say, '*Arigato*'; and in Philippines you say, '*Salamat*'..." Joshua bragged about his sudden multilingual abilities. The girls clapped looking proud of Joshua and cheering him for sounding like an expert as he pronounced the words of gratitude in various ways. "Congratulations, Josh! You said those "thank you" words very well," I complimented him.

"*Grazie*," Joshua said tilting his chin intentionally in a teasing way.

"*Prego*," I smiled in response.

"Wow, you know Italian, Dad?" Joshua asked in surprise.

"Of course," I smiled again and gave him a wink.

"So what did you learn about Thanksgiving Day, Josh?" I asked.

"Well, Dad, I learned that it all began in November of 1623. After the crops were harvested and gathered, Governor William Bradford told everyone in the Pilgrim colony to gather and give thanks to God Almighty for the plentiful harvest," Joshua became more enthusiastic about his new discovery.

"Why do we celebrate it, then?" I asked, trying to find out if he truly understood the meaning of gratitude.

"As I recall from what I have read, Dad," Josh stated, "Congress of the United States proclaimed National Days of Thanksgiving to God. Later on, when George Washington became the US president, he declared that Thursday of February 19, 1795 be the National Day of Thanksgiving. Later on, President Abraham Lincoln proclaimed that we celebrate Thanksgiving Day every last Thursday of November. All Americans give thanks to God for all the blessings during Thanksgiving Day," Joshua replied.

"You are right about the history of Thanksgiving, Josh," I agreed. "The reason why we celebrate it is not only because it is declared by law. Expressing gratitude has a positive impact on our lives. It is like charging your *Invisible Magnet* with more power to attract good things into your life," I added, in a mystical tone of voice.

"Really, Dad?" Sa'de asked, looking amazed at the thought of her *Invisible Magnet* attracting more positive things into her life through the expression of gratitude.

"That is interesting, Dad," Hannah smiled at the thought.

"I agree. It is totally interesting to really understand the true meaning of gratitude. When you do, you unlock the mystery of happiness, but you also attract positive energy into your body and mind, making your *Invisible Magnet* attract more blessings and more good things. Your *Invisible Magnet,* or your positive thoughts, will give you the opportunity to express gratitude. This, in turn, will push your magnet closer to the source of all good things: God. Remember that whatever you think about often—and that includes whatever you are thankful for--will bring about more good things," I explained in the most simple way I could.

"Thank you, Dad. Now, I understand the true meaning of Thanksgiving. It is to appreciate a lot of good things including the blessings that we have in our lives, and it is also a way of expressing gratitude to God. I think our past presidents proclaimed a national day for us to celebrate it together and express gratitude in many ways we can. But every day, we can always be thankful for what we have," Joshua concluded.

"And we do not just use our *Invisible Magnet* to attract good things that we do not have yet. We can also use it to think of the things we have that we can be thankful for," Sa'de added as she took the ice cream from the refrigerator.

"That way, we naturally attract more and more blessings and good things. When our thoughts are mostly about the things that we are thankful for, we feel happy and enthusiastic. Therefore, we perform better. When we do better, we become closer to success! Awesome, Dad!" Hannah beamed and took her first spoonful of ice cream.

"*Salamat,* Daddy!" Sa'de beamed.

"*Xie Xie*, Dad!" Hannah added.

"*Gamsahamnida,* Dad!" Joshua proudly said.

"*Chuhnman-ehyo*," I said winking.

"What was that?" Sa'de and Hannah chimed in unison full of amazement.

"That is great! You know Korean too, Dad? Wow!" Joshua looked even more proud when he realized I knew a lot of other languages.

Thanksgiving, Happiness, and Success

My family and I spent Thanksgiving Day doing charity work by serving Thanksgiving meals in a homeless shelter. It was Hannah's birthday wish to feed the homeless during Thanksgiving Day. The funds they raised during the barn dance were used to prepare the meals and loot bags for giveaways. She was genuinely happy to help those who are less fortunate. Sa'de and Joshua were glad to distribute food bags to the homeless. The shelter was filled with the spirit of gratitude that day. We left the place with a feeling of contentment and happiness. Nothing can be more fulfilling than a simple thank you from someone whom you have been able to help. It was great to see some of them shedding tears of joy upon receiving food from children who were there to help.

Thanksgiving dinner came. My family and I went out for a hearty meal. Sonia came home to celebrate Thanksgiving with us. Hannah, Sa'de, and Joshua thanked their mom for taking time from her studies to be home with the family.

"Use your *Invisible Magnet* properly so that The Law of Attraction will lead you to success. Always be grateful for what you have every day, and remember those people who have less. Know that I love you for who, and what you are," Mom said and hugged the kids.

I could think of only one word that time: Happiness.

Mind Exercise 1: Book of Names

Write down the full names, birthdays, contact numbers, and addresses of those people you are thankful for.

Names
Birthdays
Contact Number
Address

Mind Exercise 2: Postcards

Write thank you letters or notes to the top ten people in your list. Mail them postcards or send a note or letter to each of them on their next birthday.

Paste one post card you want to send to yourself here.

Mind Exercise 3: Vision Board

A Vision Board is a poster or board decorated with drawings, writing, photos and magazine cut-outs to help you visualize what you want to be, have or do in your life. Create a collage containing images and/or words that represent the things that you would like in your life. Paste photos of those who will give you happy memories.

Planning and Preparation

Brainstorm below all the things you would like to attract to yourself. If you can't think of anything then start by counting the things you don't like and then think of the opposite or alternative, or, list the things you do like or already have and think about how they could be better or improved.

Summary

When you are down and everything seems to be going wrong, remember to stop what you are doing and reflect on your thoughts and emotions at the time. Are you having bad thoughts or unhappy feelings? Then guess what? That is exactly what you are attracting to yourself! Take some time out to cheer up and get refocused on what you love and want in life- instead of all that bad stuff. There are always 'ups' and 'downs' in life but you need to focus on the good things in order to attract more good things to you you're your *Invisible Magnet*.

A good way to think about the not so nice stuff in life is to think of them as obstacles or challenges in your way of achieving your hearts desires. Overcoming these life trials will help you grow as a person. There is always a way up if you are willing to look for it. If you are having trouble staying positive you may want to try looking at your Vision Board for inspiration, writing on a piece of paper all the things you are grateful for, or do something that makes you happy like hanging out with friends or giving Mom or Dad a hug.

Think positively!

Marshmallow Tower - game about focus - keeping the goal + intention in mind - Nursery children - always started with the marshmallow - the focus was the marshmallow - adults - it was the spaghetti - build the structure in the hope it would hold the marshmallow.

"You create your own universe as you go along."

~ Winston Churchill ~

Printed in Great Britain
by Amazon

21061321R00068